MINDSET AND PRACTICE
IN
ENTREPRENEURSHIP

**MARK
BEN**

TABLE OF CONTENTS

Introduction

Chapter 1: Meaning of Entrepreneurship and its types.

Chapter 2: Entrepreneurial mindset

Chapter 3: Entrepreneurial practice

Chapter 4: Conclusion

INTRODUCTION

Entrepreneurship is regarded as a transition that frequently entails greater risk than is common when starting a business and may also contain ideals that go beyond purely material ones.

An entrepreneur is someone who creates and/or finances one or more businesses, bearing the most of the risks and earning the majority of the rewards. Starting a business is a practice of entrepreneurship. The entrepreneur is generally regarded as an inventor who develops novel ideas for goods, services, companies, and operating procedures.

The process of founding, launching, and running a new firm, which is typically comparable to a small business, is known as entrepreneurship. It may also be described as having the ability and willingness to plan ahead and successfully handle the risks associated with a business endeavour in order to make a profit.

People who launch these enterprises are typically referred to as entrepreneurs. Although starting and running a business are at the heart of most definitions of entrepreneurship, many start-up businesses fail because of a variety of factors, such as "lack of funding, poor business decisions, government policies, an economic crisis, lack of market demand, or a combination of all of these."

CHAPTER 1

The creation or extraction of economic value is referred to as entrepreneurship. This definition identifies entrepreneurship as a transition that frequently entails greater risk than is common when starting a business and may also involve values other than just financial gain.

A person who starts and/or invests in one or more enterprises, taking on the majority of the risks and reaping the majority of the gains, is referred to as an entrepreneur. Starting a business is a practice of entrepreneurship. Entrepreneurs are generally seen as innovators who can come up with novel ideas for goods, services, businesses, and operating procedures.

According to more specific definitions, entrepreneurship is the process of creating, starting, and operating a new company, which is frequently similar to a small business. It can also be defined as the "capacity and willingness to develop, organize and effectively manage a company venture's risks in order to turn a profit.

The term "entrepreneur" is widely used to describe those who launch thesex businesses. While most definitions of entrepreneurship center on starting and operating businesses, because starting a business involves significant risks, many start-up businesses fail for a variety of reasons, including "lack of funding, poor business decisions, government policies, an economic crisis, lack of market demand, or a combination of all of these."

An organization that has the capacity to transform discoveries or technological advancements into goods and services is referred to as an entrepreneur in the realm of economics.

In this view, entrepreneurship refers to both established companies' and new businesses' actions.

Apparently, Christopher According to Rea and Nicolai Volland, cultural entrepreneurship refers to the activities and sectors of the creative economy and is defined as "practices of individual and collective agency marked by movement between artistic professions and modalities of cultural output." Rea and Volland define three different categories of cultural entrepreneurs in their book The Business of Culture (2015): "cultural . personalities," who "built their own personal brand of creativity as a cultural authority and used it to establish and sustain various cultural enterprises"; "tycoons," who "entrepreneurs who built substantial clout in the cultural sphere by forging synergies between their industrial, cultural, political, and philanthropic interests" In the 2000s, storytelling was investigated as a cultural entrepreneurship topic.

Some have stated that businesspeople should be viewed as "talented cultural operators" who take advantage of market possibilities and fresh funding by using stories to establish credibility. Others have come to the conclusion that there has to be a "story turn" in the study of cultural entrepreneurship.

Kinds of Entrepreneurship

Ethnic

In the United States and Europe, self-employed business owners who are members of racial or ethnic minorities are referred to as "ethnic entrepreneurs"[citation needed]. The experiences and tactics used by ethnic entrepreneurs as they attempt Scholarly research on how to economically integrate into mainstream American or European society is not new. Classic examples include Chinese and Jewish traders and merchants in large American cities in the 19th and early 20th centuries. and West Coast Japanese small business operators (farmers, restaurateurs, and shopkeepers).

In the 2010s, studies on ethnic entrepreneurship focused on Chinese business owners in Chinatowns around the nation as well as Cuban business owners in Miami. Racial and ethnic differences in self-employment and business ownership still exist in the United States, despite the fact that entrepreneurship gives these groups many opportunities for economic advancement. A recent statistical examination of U.S. census data reveals that whites are more likely than Asians, African-Americans, and Latinos to be self-employed in high prestige, lucrative industries, despite the abundance of success tales of Asian entrepreneurs.

Feminist

An individual who uses entrepreneurship to apply feminist principles and practices with the intention of enhancing the girls' and women's quality of life and wellbeing. Many people accomplish this by starting enterprises "for women, by women." Feminist entrepreneurs are motivated to start businesses because they are committed to the principles of cooperation, equality, and respect. Both liberation and empowerment may come about as a result of these efforts.

Institutional

The collaborative element of entrepreneurship has been highlighted by British economist Edith Penrose, who was born in the United StatesShe makes the point that modern businesses must combine their human resources in order to efficiently identify and develop commercial chances. Paul DiMaggio, a sociologist, established this theory and asserts that "new institutions emerge when organized persons with sufficient resources [institutional entrepreneurs] recognize in them a need that they can fill a chance to satisfy interests that they value highly." The belief has been used extensively.

Millennial

The term "millennial entrepreneur" describes a business owner who belongs to the generation known as millennials, or Generation Y, which includes those born between about 1981 and 1996.

This generation, which includes early Gen Xers and baby boomers, was raised in an era of digital technology and mass media. Entrepreneurs from the millennial generation are very knowledgeable about how new technologies and business models can be used in real-world settings. Facebook's founder Mark Zuckerberg and other young business people have started a number of revolutionary enterprises. Despite the belief that millennials would succeed, new research has shown that this is not the case. When millennials who are and are not self-employed are compared, the latter group outperforms the former. This is because they were raised by a different generation and have a different mindset than their parents. The state of the economy, student loan debt, and the difficulties associated with regulatory compliance are a few of the obstacles faced by entrepreneurs.

Nascent

A budding entrepreneur is someone who is just starting out in business. This viewpoint suggests that the aspiring entrepreneur may be seen as seizing an opportunity, or the possibility to provide new services or products, target new markets, or produce greater wealth. e productive manufacturing techniques in a way that is profitableHowever, until such a company is actually started, the prospect is still only a business concept. Alternatively said, Perceptual in nature, the pursued opportunity is supported by the aspiring entrepreneur's personal convictions regarding the viability of the venture objectives he or she desires to achieve.

Its foresight and worth can only be gradually confirmed in the context of the actions the nascent entrepreneur takes to establish the venture. In the end, these actions may lead down a path that the nascent entrepreneur finds to be neither appealing nor feasible or may cause a (viable) business to emerge. In this sense, the fledgling endeavor can progress through time either toward being abandoned or toward effectively emerging as a functional entity.

An illustration of behavior-based categorization is the contrast between novice, serial, and portfolio entrepreneurs. Additional instances include the (related) studies on startup events. sequences. Developing entrepreneurship that places more emphasis on the chain of events that lead to the creation of a new enterprise than on the lone act of seizing an opportunity. An activity (or sequence of activities) and a person's motivation to form an opportunity belief, as well as an activity (or sequence of activities) and the knowledge required to form an opportunity belief, are all related in ways that will help separate entrepreneurial action into its fundamental sub-activities. With the aid of this research, researchers will be able to begin formulating a theory of the micro-foundations of entrepreneurial action.

Researchers that are interested in emerging entrepreneurship sometimes place greater emphasis on the chain of acts that lead to the formation of new ventures than on a single act of opportunity exploitation. In fact, aspiring business owners engage in a variety of entrepreneurial activities, including behaviors that help them and others understand their company better.For example, new business owners usually search for and purchase properties and equipment, seek and obtain financial backing, set up legal entities, build teams, and commit their full time and energy to their businesses attention to their venture.

Project-based

Project entrepreneurs are those who organize or create temporary groupings of people repeatedly. These are organizations with short lifespans that are committed to achieving a single objective or goal and dissolve quickly after the project is completedProject-based enterprises are prevalent in a number of different industries, including sound recording, film production, software development, television production, new media, and construction. The demand to "rewire" and modify these temporary businesses in order to satisfy the needs of new projects and possibilities that arise is what theoretically distinguishes project-entrepreneurs. If a project entrepreneur employed a specific strategy and team for one project, they might need to alter the business strategy or team for a later project.

Project entrepreneurs regularly deal with the challenges and responsibilities related to the entrepreneurial process.

Finding the ideal opportunity to launch the project enterprise and putting together the best team to take advantage of that opportunity are, in fact, the two most significant hurdles faced by project-based entrepreneurs. Project entrepreneurs must access a wide variety of information in order to take advantage of new investment opportunities in order to overcome the first hurdle.

For the second challenge to be overcome, a cooperative team must be put together. This team must be able to work quickly to minimize the possibility of performance being negatively impacted while also fitting well with the project's unique challenges.
Entrepreneurs can work on projects together with business students to gain analysis on their ideas.

CHAPTER 2

What is the mindset of an entrepreneur?
An entrepreneurial mindset is a way of thinking that enables you to get beyond challenges, act quickly, and take responsibility for your outcomes. You must constantly work to develop your abilities, learn from your errors, and implement your ideas. Anyone who is prepared to put in the effort can cultivate an entrepreneurial mindset.

Entrepreneurial Components

One: Risk

Understanding and reducing risk is the primary motivation for actions in business and in life. Risk is not only the reason why people avoid taking risks; paradoxically, it is also the reason why people take risks. For example, gamblers enjoy the rush of adrenaline they get from tossing the dice or waiting for the next card because it fuels their desire to move on to the next riskhazard or gamble.

We all take risks occasionally—driving at 85 mph when the speed limit is 70, for example—and we all experience a small rush when we take a chance because it adds some spice to life.

Strangely, not taking a chance can have a long-term depressive impact on your life, leading to an annoying circle of questions in your head when things go wrong or are going well in your life: why, oh why, did you not take that associate job in Sydney back in 2001? If you had, you wouldn't be waiting in this depressing NHS office in Clapham on a gloomy Tuesday in February. Unthankful, boring, and stinky patients fill the waiting room to capacity…

Your life is shaped by how you see risk. You don't need to take chances to be happy, but if you want to be an entrepreneur, you must do it frequently.

"You will be more disappointed in the things you didn't accomplish than the ones you did in twenty years." Twain, Mark.

List all the consequences of taking a risk objectively as the first step in understanding risk. Start by identifying the purpose for taking the risk in the first place.

List the costs, the energy wasted, and the effect on morale if it completely fails. And now, here is the List of all the unanticipated effects of taking the risk; this is the tough part.

Is the list lengthy? Great. Because you have considered every single potential result or effect, you have now placed yourself in a position where you can manage or mitigate the risk. You have the power.

The following step is to create a fix or a workaround for each potential scenario. Yes, I realize it's tedious, but I guarantee you'll feel entirely different in the end about taking the risk—no matter how big.

Realistically, a full failure of a risk would be relatively uncommon. It's very likely that just 40% of the anticipated new patients included in your strategy really arrive.

Two: Motivating

The question at hand is whether you want to be a "Steady Eddy" or whether you want to take a chance and stand out.

Getting this part of your thinking straight is crucial to how you should approach your business. No matter how entrepreneurial your personality and behavioral style is, if you don't truly want it, you won't be able to get it. And let's face it, we need Steady Eddies, like the pilot of the flight that will carry your family and you on vacation.

Three: Ongoing construction and improvement

It was challenging for me to think of a better phrase, but constant building and development captures the idea of combining numerous, seemingly unconnected pieces or circumstances to create something larger.

Jeff Bezos, the individual responsible for the founding of Amazon, is the ideal example of this attitude. The internet and e-retailing were already invented before Bezos entered the market, despite the fact that he owns the largest e-retailer in the world.

His plan did not include the rationale for Amazon's success; initially, the company's business model revolved entirely around tax evasion. Online merchants in the US are not required to collect sales tax in states where they do not have a physical presence, which gives Amazon a considerable price advantage. advantage.

Bezos, though, was not content to stop there. When he met a man who introduced him to predictive analytics, he decided to try integrating it into his product. This turned out to be a wise choice.

We all enjoy the thought of being presented yet another book on our specialized but favored subject as consumers. As an online store, it's the ideal differentiator that simultaneously boosts sales, makes shopping memorable, and fosters exceptional loyalty and lifelong customer value. Amazon took off as a result.

The need to keep building opens up more and more options. It's similar to a practice opening on the weekend for emergency care and finding a sizable number of new clients who would gladly pay a higher rate to see the hygienist on a Sunday afternoon.

Four: Take pleasure in your blunders.

Be prepared to make lots of blunders throughout your professional career. A practice's management is not an exact science. Remember Sir Clive Sinclair's C5, which regrettably became the biggest laughingstock of the 1980s, or Coca-disastrous Cola's introduction of the "new" Coke in 1985?

You'll practice this year and make a ton of mistakes. You must make a change right away, even though it will be difficult, once you realize that the ingenious new pay plan you made with your star associate won't work for you. Although it is annoying, failing quickly is actually not all that horrible; you will get over it. Slow failure is dangerous and incredibly disheartening. Always have a plan B and a plan C in place before making changes, since this will boost your confidence at the very least.

Entrepreneurs commit a staggering number of errors. They don't dwell on it; instead, they quickly move on to the solution or the next concept, but they never stop learning.

Five: Quick learning

When something goes wrong, swiftly disassemble it to identify the problematic component. Did you fail to convince the team of this? Did you get the patient's needs wrong? What was the component that failed and caused the plane to go down? What specific aspect did people truly like when things went well, and how might you build on it?

Entrepreneurs pick things up quickly, but they always communicate their successes and failures with the team to move the boat forward.

Sixth: Adjust to changes.

Four years from now, I'll be a zero.

Nokia was at its best and virtually unbeatable in 2007. It had been "the" stylish brand for the past ten years. It had an estimated 32% of the market for feature phones worldwide, with a healthy average margin of 36%. However, Nokia was slow to enter the smartphone market, leaving a huge gap. Apple and, more recently, Samsung's unstoppable power quickly occupied the area, and currently rule.

With an annual margin of 18% and an 8.6% market share, Nokia ended the year 2012. It produced a variety of excellent products in response to the market's quick transition, but it was already too late. Nokia is currently engaged in a rearguard action after Apple and Samsung had seized the market, and it will remain thus until the next great mobile invention upends the market and forces change once more.

The flames of creativity frequently die when a business expands, or when a practice reaches its pinnacle (in the view of the owner), it fails to innovate or take any chances by seizing market opportunities, like a new pharmacy opening two doors down. What kind of entrepreneur profits from that?

Seventh: Exercise good judgment.

Entrepreneurs frequently have the delusion that they are the only ones who can complete tasks and make things truly perfect. Naturally, this is utterly insane and reduces their efficiency significantly.

There is no exception to the 80/20 rule. However success is defined, typically 20% of your activities generates 80% of your success.

When the proper individual could accomplish that task in three minutes, spending hours trying to sync your diary between your laptop and desktop is foolish when you might have instead spent the day immediately expanding your company.

Be shrewd, be aware of your strengths and weaknesses, and play to your advantages. Carefully Develop or find individuals that will fill in for your weaknesses while enhancing your strengths.

Determine when you are most productive. Everyone has a time when they are most productive and able to think clearly. For me, that time is between 6 and 11 in the morning.

Above all else, the entrepreneur knows himself and treats himself like a machine. He always makes sure he is in peak physical and mental condition, and he may occasionally show signs of hypochondria.

CHAPTER 3
Practice Of Entrepreneurship

The practice of entrepreneurship has several facets. Others may define it as the creation of a cutting-edge business, the invention or re-invention of a good, a service, or a method, or the creation of remedies for social, cultural, or environmental problems. For some, it is simply the pursuit of an opportunity. Entrepreneurship or entrepreneurial behavior is fundamentally a mindset.

The practice of entrepreneurship encompasses a variety of viewpoints, including management, sociology, psychology, and economics.

Before you launch a business, here are some ways to practice entrepreneurship.

The business world is a contact sport. It cannot be taught in a classroom or via a book. Entrepreneurship skills are mostly acquired through hands-on experience and trial-and-error learning.

But you don't have to launch a company to start using your entrepreneurial abilities. While you are at school or employed by a huge company, you can carry out a variety of jobs that will enable you to practice the art of entrepreneurship.

Establishing your desired outcomes is the first step in effective practicing. You will only be able to increase your individual skills by accident if you don't know which ones you want to focus on.

Practice Purposefully
"There is no glory in practice, but there is no glory without practice."

-Unknown

Without committing all of your resources to one project, you can develop your entrepreneurial talents by engaging in the following seven activities. Concentrate on the workouts that will improve you. most unpleasant, instead of putting effort into developing your abilities.

1. Provide Advice to a Startup

"As you learn, you will also be able to teach others. As you learn, you will also be able to teach others.
-Latin saying

I'm not qualified to counsel a startup, you may be thinking. I'm reading this essay for that reason. Not to teach, but to learn. Great. When you are made to teach, there is no better way to learn.

Regardless of where you are in the entrepreneurial development process, there are a lot of smart, enthusiastic people that are slightly ahead of you. Give advice to a high school entrepreneur club if you are in college. Mentor college students if you have just graduated. Work with a group of prospective business owners if you are an experienced executive.

2. Improve Your Individual Pitch

"You bleed less in fights the more you perspire in training."
-Author Richard Marcinko

One of an entrepreneur's most important abilities is networking. Aim to establish at least five significant contacts with individuals who can help the startup you are advising by constantly entering a room of strangers

By incorporating your Personal Pitch into your networking encounters, you can easily avoid awkward pauses. You should include the following three things in your pitch.

Your interests, experiences, education, and the reasons you are so dang fascinating make up who you are.

Your grandiose, exciting entrepreneurial ideas are where you are going.

How you want to get there, including your immediate and long-term plans for realizing your goals.

Even more of a reason to practice networking if it makes you uncomfortable, as it does for many individuals. As with all skills, as you get more adept at networking, you will feel less anxious both during practice sessions and during actual games.

You can use the company's pitch instead of your own if you're networking to help a business you're mentoring.

3. Business It

"Stop practicing once you have it down. until you can execute it right, practice.

-Unknown

Look for areas at your place of employment From nothing, something can be made. Launch a project that will wow your boss by using little to no resources yet having a significant influence on your company.

What aspects of our operations would an entrepreneur modify if they were recruited by us? then put into practice any recommendations you come up with. Don't worry, you may make amends later on when you highlight the advantageous effects your endeavor had on your business.

Do something risqué while a member of a club or student organization if you're a student. Whatever you do, it should be audacious and force you to use all of your startup skills. For example, you could start a community service project or raise a small venture fund to finance student businesses.

4. Keep a journal of your ideas because "practice makes brains stronger"

-Sam Snead, PGA Tour player

Epiphanies are uncommon, as Stephen Johnson illustrates in Where Good Ideas Come From. The majority of innovations come about as a result of little ideas slamming against larger ones. It is advantageous to write down your daily thoughts in order to remember them later and mix them with other hunches.

These notebooks, originally known as Commonplace Books, were utilized by inquisitive, deep thinkers during the 17th and 18th centuries, including Milton, Bacon, Locke, Franklin, and Darwin. Evernote, Google Keep, and other services are used by modern entrepreneurs to record and organize their hunches.

5. Establish A Second Business

"Practice makes the difference between average and remarkable"

-Pianist Vladimir Horowitz

As mentioned in Mini-ventures Build Entrepreneurial Muscle, a number of significant businesses have spawned from businesses founded by individuals who were enrolled in school and held full-time employment.

Even if your mini-venture doesn't grow into a major company, it will serve as a useful testing ground for your entrepreneurial skills.

6. "You earn your trophies at practice, you just pick them up when you perform," is a quote from the song "Don't Throw Up, Speak Up."

-Unknown

Entrepreneurs need to have the ability to convince and sway people, frequently in front of others. By offering to deliver presentations at work, school, or non-profit groups, you can hone this talent. You can also join organizations like Toastmasters, whose main goal is to develop its members' public speaking skills and confidence.

Similar to networking, aggressively practice your way to proficiency if public speaking makes you uneasy.

7. Get a coach
You "play" as you "train."

-Unknown

It is challenging to practice by yourself. It's difficult to objectively determine the talents you are advancing in and where you should concentrate your practice time in addition to being difficult to stay motivated.

Similar to athletes, business owners gain a lot from having a coach in the form of a supportive mentor. It is time well spent to cultivate a mentor connection, as stated in You're Never Too Old (Or Successful) For A Mentor.

8. Innovation

Every successful business person should be inventive in some way and be able to foresee the market's need for a particular commodity or service since this sets them apart from other businesspeople and makes their ventures even more successful. When a businessperson is inventive, he or she notices fresh opportunities emerging in unexpected locations. For instance, when the founders of OLA Cabs, Bhavish Aggarwal and Ankit Bhati, recognized the expanding demand for acceptable and economical public transportation in India, they were inspired to start OLA Cabs. OLA is currently valued at US$6.5 billion, with quite 1.5 million riders on a regular basis. So be it forever ingenious, creative, and capable of spotting opportunities that others miss.

9 Organization

One of the essential elements of a successful entrepreneurial venture is organization. Without structure, everything will become chaotic and unmanageable, which will further result in losses, a decline in goodwill, dissatisfied clients, and staff members who may leave the company. Therefore, it is crucial for the company to have an honest organizational structure that outlines who will perform a specific duty and how that activity would be carried out.

10 Making Decisions

Entrepreneurs must carefully analyze each option because they make many decisions each day, are frequently exposed to danger, and should always learn from their prior errors.

Making decisions might be a talent that comes naturally to entrepreneurs who take big risks in business. Instead of focusing on snap judgments, an entrepreneur should prioritize decisions that take time to consider. A good businessperson weighs the advantages and disadvantages in visiting another company. Because they are aware of what is happening in the corporate zone, an honest leader will always consult his staff. Experience, intuition, intelligence, knowledge of the corporate environment, effective listening skills, and the capacity to react when necessary are all necessary for good decision-making.

11 Taker of Risk

A business owner must realize that risk cannot be totally removed, thus he or she must also be ready for its effects. It's possible that customers won't appear to be happy with the products or services received, or the competition may offer the same thing at a lower cost and higher quality, or there may be changes in the government's policy. These many dangers can never be completely eradicated, so the entrepreneur must always be ready for them and develop a niche that allows them to be catered to. For instance, if customers aren't happy with the product, the business owner needs to find a way to improve it so that customers are happy.

12. Vision

Every great business person had a single idea that they were passionate about as a child, but over time, that enthusiasm waned. Good business people possess this energy and vision because they cannot succeed without these qualities. grow. Young business people, regrettably, often have amazing concepts that never materialize into ideas. Recognizing that many entrepreneurs fail, but what matters most is how hard they tried is a key to success. If one concept doesn't work, try another; it might be the right one for you. Don't be afraid to take risks because that's what will set you apart from the competition and give you power. Visionaries must take the steps necessary to achieve their goals. To succeed, businesspeople must embrace the paradox of the center. You can stay focused and make sure your actions are moving you in the proper path by using the vision of thinking.

CHAPTER 4
Conclusion

For me, starting a business is the most thrilling and rewarding sport imaginable; each day seems like I'm attending a brand-new celebration.

There are no magic formulas for success. It is the outcome of planning, putting in a lot of effort, and learning from mistakes. Colin Powel It would be valuable. it if your company succeeds on its first attempt, but it doesn't happen very often. However, success is largely a result of giving your all and taking lessons from your prior errors. This is not a justification for you to fail.

Every endeavor continues to be a test of success. When you do fail, though, you learn from your mistake and work harder the next time around. Deliberate practice is a unique type of practice that is organized and purposeful. While intentional practice calls for concentrated attention and is done with the specific intention of improving results, ordinary practice may involve mindless repetitions.

Skateboarding is the best parallel I can think of for this situation. It's not just mindless repetition till you understand a new trick you're learning. Every effort could be a chance to get it correct if you practice deliberately. If a trick is not successfully executed, you analyze the situation and adjust. Perhaps your body was in the wrong position, your feet weren't in the proper spot, or you were out of balance. You then adjust to that circumstance in a different way. Failure is caused by doing something badly, not only by a lack of expertise. Understanding that will enable you to take advantage of it and increase your success rate.

www.ingramcontent.com/pod-product-compliance
Lightning Source LLC
Chambersburg PA
CBHW050324220526
45465CB00005B/2122